Contents

Communities   **4**

Important people in a community   **6**

Clues from shops   **8**

Who lived here?   **10**

Who died here?   **12**

Killed or wounded in battle   **14**

Children in the past   **16**

Hilda and the birthday book   **18**

Discovering Grandfather Tom   **20**

Families on the move   **22**

Finding the Dawson family   **24**

Martha on the move   **26**

A Jewish family   **28**

Glossary   **30**

Index   **32**

CERTIFIED COPY OF AN   REGISTER OFFICE,
SOMERSET HOUSE, LONDON

The fee for this certificate is 40p.
When application is made by post, a
handling fee is payable in addition.

Application Number PAS 43498/41

Form A513 (5.32472) Dt47360.41 30,000 1270 Hw-RE-59

Registration District   City of London

1842. Marriage solemnized at 106 Shoe Lane
in the — of West London in the City of London

No.	When married	Name and surname	Age	Condition	Rank or profession	Residence at the time of marriage	Father's name and surname	Rank or profession of father
1	September 28th	George Woolf	full	Bachelor	Accountant	106 Shoe Lane	Joseph Woolf	—
		Maria Mordecai	—	Spinster	—	20 John Street Waterloo Road	Jonas Mordecai	—

Married in the Congregation of the New Synagogue according to the Rites & Ceremonies of the German & Polish Jews by me Abm Bassett Reader

This marriage was solemnized between us, { George Woolf / Maria Woolf } in the presence of us, { P Harris / Moses Levy } J L Lindenthal Registrar

CERTIFIED to be a true copy of an entry in the certified copy of a Register of Marriages in the District above mentioned.

Given at the GENERAL REGISTER OFFICE, SOMERSET HOUSE, LONDON, under the Seal of the said Office, the 24th day of August 19 71.

MA 945307

This certificate is issued in pursuance of section 65 of the Marriage Act 1949. Sub-section (3) of that section provides that any certified copy of an entry purporting to be sealed or stamped with the seal of the General Register Office shall be received as evidence of the marriage to which it relates without any further or other proof of the entry, and no certified copy purporting to have been given in the said Office shall be of any force or effect unless it is sealed or stamped as aforesaid.

CAUTION:—Any person who (1) falsifies any of the particulars on this certificate, or (2) uses a falsified certificate as true knowing it to be false, is liable to prosecution.

Communities

What is a community?

A community is a group of people who live in the same place. Communities often have shared buildings, such as a church, village hall, library, health centre and some shops. Communities do things together. They might organize a flower show or a music festival. They might have a village cricket club or a town football team.

Village communities

Small villages are really just one community. Big villages and small towns may be made up of two or three communities.

For example, the people who live either side of a railway line might make up two different communities.

City communities

Cities are made up of lots of different communities. Different areas of a city have different names. For example, Heaton and Manningham are both separate areas and communities inside the city of Bradford.

This carnival happens every year in Notting Hill, which is part of London. It is organized by local people.

What happens in a community?

There are lots of things to do in a community. Some things are special, such as festivals, and may happen once a year. Some things are more ordinary and happen every day or every week. The local hall is an important place for a community. People organize play-groups there for young children, 'Keep Fit' classes, and drama groups. The things that happen depend on what the people in the area want to organize.

Studying a community

There are lots of ways to find out about your community. The first part of this book tells you about some of them. The second part of this book tells you how two people used community records, and other clues, to find out about their families back in time.

These Brownies are meeting in their local hall.

LOOK OUT

Where can you go to find out what happens in your local community? Will you find this information in the village hall, or post office?

What kind of things are happening in your community?

Important people
in a **community**

Clues from foundation stones

Some important buildings, such as libraries, churches and town halls, have foundation stones. These are special stones set into the building. You will find them fairly low down, near the pavement. The foundation stone will have been specially made. It will have been set there by the local **mayor** or another important person.

Foundation stones tell us that the building must have been important at the time, even if it is not important now. They can also give us a lot of information about the place at the time the stone was laid.

Look at the foundation stone in the picture. It is set in a wall of the town hall at Colyton in Devon. It tells us that the stone was laid on 5th January, 1927. This date tells us when the town hall was built. It also tells us that the town hall **architect** (the person who planned the building) came from Exeter. What else does the foundation stone tell us?

The foundation stone of the town hall in Colyton in Devon.

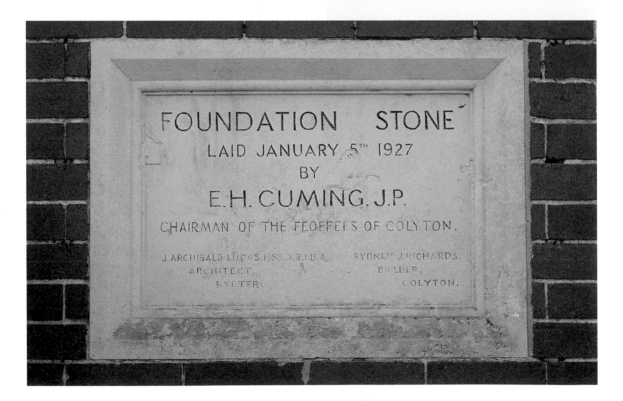

FOUNDATION STONE
LAID JANUARY 5TH 1927
BY
E.H. CUMING. J.P.
CHAIRMAN OF THE FEOFFEES OF COLYTON.

J. ARCHIBALD LUCAS F.S....F.R.I.B.A.   SYDNEY J. RICHARDS.
ARCHITECT.   BUILDER,
EXETER.   COLYTON.

This statue of Queen Victoria is in Harrogate, a town in North Yorkshire.

Clues from statues

Statues are usually models of people or animals. They are made from stone, metal or **plaster**.

Some people have statues in their gardens. These statues may be of little gnomes, animals or people. Is there a statue in a garden near you?

Statues might also be of **imaginary** people. You will see them in towns and cities, parks and gardens. They can be fun or serious.

Statues of famous people

Many towns and cities have statues of **famous** people. You might find a statue of a famous person in a market place or park, outside a church or library, or in a town square. Thousands of statues have been made of one famous person, Queen Victoria. She was queen of Great Britain between 1837 and 1901. People put up statues of Queen Victoria to show how proud they were of Great Britain with her as its queen.

LOOK OUT

See how many statues you can find of people who once lived and worked near you. What did they do to make themselves famous and important?

Clues from shops

Shopping

When you go shopping, what sort of shops do you go to? Perhaps you go to a corner shop where you can buy sweets and comics. Or perhaps you go to a big supermarket where you can choose what you want from all sorts of goods from different countries.

Supermarkets

Some shops or supermarkets in different towns or cities have the same names. Asda, Marks and Spencer, Safeway, Sainsbury's and W H Smith are all names of chains of shops. Each shop in the chain looks the same and sells the same sorts of goods. Each chain of shops is owned by one company, which decides what will be sold and at what price.

Family shops

Some shops are owned by just one family. Look at the name of the shop in the photograph. It is, or was, owned by someone called R Yates and his or her sons. By asking, you could find out if the owners today are called Yates. To find out whether the Yates family owned the shop a hundred years ago, you could look in a **street directory**.

Street directories

In the 19th century, most towns and cities had books called street directories. A modern telephone directory tells us the telephone numbers of people and places. Street directories tell us all the jobs that were done in the town, the names of the people who did the work, and the addresses of where they worked. If you use directories for the same place, but from different times, you can see how the place has changed. Some jobs may be quite new, while people may have stopped doing other jobs altogether.

A shop in Malton, North Yorkshire.

BURNLEY.

Paper Makers.

Burnley Paper Works Co., Limited, Calder Vale; J. Isherwood, manager

Paper Bag Makers.

Bibby & Baron, Finsleygate
Ellis John N. (dealer), Calder street

Pattern Maker.

Ashworth George R., Parker lane

Pawnbrokers.

Austin Thomas, 23 Parker street
Bailey Thomas, 20 Sandygate
Binns Thomas, 68 Bridge street
Brown Mrs. Ann, 7 Fleet street
Denbigh Road, 38 Parker lane
Holme Thomas, 10 Hammerton street
Kippax Jeremiah (exors. of), 10 Parker lane
Laycock Utley, 39 Hammerton street
Lord James, 6 Croft street
West Rd. H., 112 St. James street

Photographers.

Brooks David, Healey Wood road
Greenwood James, 12 Todmorden road
Hargreaves James, 3 Hattersley street
Holden Joseph, 55 Master street
Lancaster Samuel, 69a Curzon street
Sutcliffe Frederick C., 40 Manchester rd.
Wilkinson Joseph, 59 Albion street

Plasterers.

Coupe John, 10 Gas street
Rawlinson Rt., 8 Union street
Shuttleworth John, 55 Curzon st.
Smith Robert, 121 Manchester road
Thompson John, 29 Padiham road
Wood Isaac, 18 Oxford road

Plumbers, Glaziers, &c.

Berry Thomas, 21 Curzon street
Brooks John, 34 Trafalgar street
Hargreaves James R., 22 Hargreaves street
Lord Henry, 8 Oxford road
Lord John, 29 Howe street
Owen William, 48 Yorkshire street
Shoesmith James, 79 Manchester road
West Thomas, 25 Yorkshire street
Whitehead Thomas, 69 Westgate and
        2 Hall street

Printers (Letterpress).

Bulcock John, 11 Coal street
Burghope & Strange (and engravers and lithographers),
        50 James street
Burnley Gazette Co., Limited, St. James row
Clegg John, 92 St. James street
Frankland George (and lithographer),
        Bull street
Grant James (and lithographer),
        14 Manchester road
Nuttall James & Co., Bridge street
Waddington William, 40 St. James st.

Professors of Music.

Hudson George F., 119 Manchester rd.
Lonsdale Henry, 19 Todmorden road
Myers Stephen, 64 St. James street
Nuttall William, 215 Padiham road
Pollard James, 140 Cumberland place,
        Manchester road
Pollard Thomas, Market place
Simpson Thomas, 23 Manchester road

Provision Merchants.

Dickinson Alfred, 24 Market place
Harrison George 12 and 14 St. James street
Hoghton Thomas, 66 St. James street
Manley Matthew, 1 Market hall
Thompson James, Liverpool house,
        62 St. James street
Ward Jonathan, Railway street

This is part of the street directory for Burnley, in Lancashire, in the 1880s. Do you know what all the jobs are? Which ones are still done today?

LOOK OUT

See how many shop names you can find which tell you that they are, or were, run by a family.

Who lived here?

Homes today

Who lives in the houses and flats around you? Some houses may have had lots of different families living in them, one after the other. Some houses may have been lived in by the same family for many years. You probably know who lives next door to you. But you probably do not know who lives in every house in your street, and you almost certainly do not know who lives in every house in your community!

What is a census?

Some people know who lives in every house in the country. Every ten years the government sends a special form to every house in the country. The people living in the house have to fill in the form. They have to write down how many people live there, what their names and ages are, and where they were born. This is called a **census**.

The information from the census is kept secret for 100 years from everyone except the government. This is because most people want this sort of information about themselves and their families to be kept private. But the government needs the information so that they can, for example, work out how many schools and hospitals need to be built.

These houses were built in London in the 1930s. We would have to wait until the year 2031 or 2041 to read the census which would tell us who lived in them at the time they were built.

Parish or Township of *Habergham Eaves*	Ecclesiastical District of *the Holy Trinity*	City or Borough of	Town of	Village of	
Name of Street, Place, or Road, and Name or No. of House	Name and Surname of each Person who abode in the house, on the Night of the 30th March, 1851	Relation to Head of Family	Condition	Age of Males / Females	Rank, Profession, or Occupation	Where Born	Whether Blind, or Deaf-and-Dumb

No.	Street	Name	Relation	Condition	M	F	Occupation	Where Born	
	Smithy Shop	George Richardson	Son	U	30		Machine Maker Iron Works	Lancaster Wigan	
190	3 Mason Terrace	James Barnes	Head	Mar	29		General Labourer	" Accrington	
		Isabella "	Wife	Mar		27	Power Loom Weaver (Cotton)	" Reedley Hollows	
		Maria Simpson	Cousin	U		17	" " " (")	" Barrowford	
		Sarah Parkinson	Lodger	U		24	" " " (")	" Burnley	
191	2 Mason Terrace	Thompson Hargreaves	Head	Mar	34		Cotton Piece Looker	" Barrowford	
		Mary A. "	Wife	Mar		33		" Habergham Eaves	
		Sarah A. "	Dau			8	Scholar	" Habergham Eaves	
		Elizabeth "	Dau			6		" "	
		James "	Son			2		" "	
192	4 Mason Terrace	Jeremiah Brown	Head	Mar	40		Blacksmith	" "	
		Susannah "	Wife	Mar		40		" "	
		Ann "	Dau	U		17	Power Loom Weaver (Cotton)	" "	
		James "	Son		12		Blacksmith (app)	" Rawtenstall	
		Elizabeth "	Dau			9	Scholar	" Hab: Eaves	
		Susannah "	Dau			6		" "	
193	6 Mason Terrace	John Haste	Head	Mar	34		Worsted Machine Maker	York Bradford	
		Hannah "	Wife	Mar		28		" "	
194		John Holgate	Head	Mar	40		Overlooker in Cotton Mill	Lancashire Roughlee	
		Grace "	Wife	Mar		42		York Kelbrook	
Total of Houses	14 U B						Total of Persons..	7 / 13	

Censuses in the 19th century

The first census for the whole of Britain was taken in 1801. Few people could read or write then. The government could not send out forms for people to read and fill in. So they sent people, called **enumerators**, to every house. It was their job to find out who lived there, what jobs they did, how old they were and where they were born. The questions became more complicated as time went by.

By looking at the old census returns, we can find out a lot about who lived in a particular town or village.

This is part of the 1851 census for Habergham Eaves in Lancashire.

LOOK OUT

What sort of work was done by a weaver and an overlooker? What was a power loom?

Who died here?

Old gravestones

If you visit an old **graveyard** you will be able to find out a lot about people's lives in the past. The gravestones tell you who is buried there. They tell you when people were born and when they died. They may say where people were born and what the names of their parents were. They might also tell you what jobs the people did. In some graves, there is more than one person buried. Often, a wife and husband will be buried together. Children, particularly if the children died when they were young, were usually buried with their parents.

Death and disease

Some gravestones tell you what the person died from. You may find a lot of gravestones where the people died from the same **disease** at more or less the same time. An **epidemic** is when a lot of people catch the same illness at the same time. In Britain in 1832–3, 1848–9, 1853–4, and again in 1866, there were epidemics of **cholera**. Thousands of people died. Thousands died too, in 1918, when 'flu swept through Britain.

This gravestone is at Kenton, near Exmouth, in Devon.

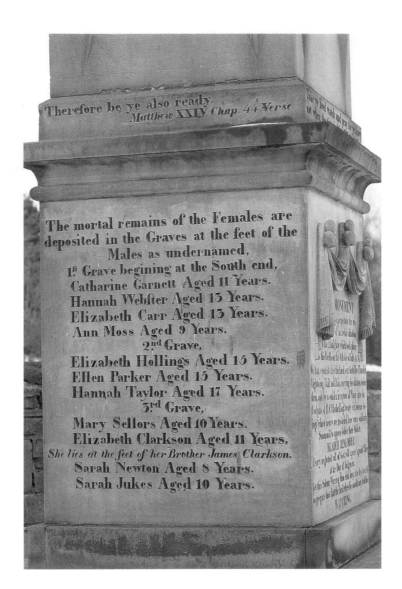

Part of the memorial in Silkstone churchyard, near Barnsley, in South Yorkshire.

The inscription on the memorial reads:

Therefore be ye also ready.
Matthew XXIV Chap. 44 Verse

The mortal remains of the Females are deposited in the Graves at the feet of the Males as undernamed,
1st Grave begining at the South end,
Catharine Garnett Aged 11 Years.
Hannah Webster Aged 13 Years.
Elizabeth Carr Aged 13 Years.
Ann Moss Aged 9 Years.
2nd Grave,
Elizabeth Hollings Aged 15 Years.
Ellen Parker Aged 15 Years.
Hannah Taylor Aged 17 Years.
3rd Grave,
Mary Sellors Aged 10 Years.
Elizabeth Clarkson Aged 11 Years,
She lies at the feet of her Brother James Clarkson.
Sarah Newton Aged 8 Years.
Sarah Jukes Aged 10 Years.

Disasters

Look at the photograph on this page and you will see a **memorial** to a disaster. Mr Clarke owned some coal-mines in Silkstone, a village near Barnsley in South Yorkshire. On 4th July, 1838, after a terrible storm, the mines flooded. Twenty-eight people drowned, and most of them were children.

This memorial to the disaster tells us what happened. It also tells us the names of the children and their ages. But it tells us something else, too. It tells us that girls and boys were allowed to work down mines; it also tells us that some of the children were as young as seven years old.

Parliament acts

In 1842, **Parliament** passed a law. This said that no boys under the age of ten could work down coal-mines. Girls and women were not allowed to work down mines at all.

LOOK OUT

Gravestones are usually made from local materials. What are the gravestones in your local graveyard made from? Where did the material come from?

Killed or wounded in battle

What is a war memorial?

Most villages and towns have a war **memorial**. They have all the names of the people who once lived in the community and who were killed fighting in the First World War (1914–18) and the Second World War (1939–45).

Local people wanted to remember the names of those who had been killed in the two terrible wars. They did not want the people who came after them to forget, either. This is why there are so many war memorials throughout the country.

What else do war memorials tell us?

Look at the surnames of the young men on your local war memorial. Were any of them from the same family?

Some war memorials have the dates on which the young men were killed. You could write down the dates, and later check what battles were happening at that time. Sometimes most of the men in one town joined the same army **regiment**. This could have been because the town had a special link with that regiment. Or it could be because the young men joined a **Pals regiment** which was specially formed by the army so that friends could fight together.

This is a war memorial in Padiham, Lancashire.

LOOK OUT

Most of the names on war memorials are men's names. Does this mean that no women were killed fighting?

The Observer & Times

No. 3,260.   THE OBSERVER AND TIMES, SATURDAY, JULY 22, 1916.   One Halfpenny

WOUNDED "PALS."

PTE. WILLIAM JOHNSON (Accrington) of 35, Park-street, is in a London hospital recovering from shell shock. An employee of Messrs. Howard and Bullough's, he is on the roll of honour at the New Jerusaleum school.

LANCE-CORPL. W. BRIGGS (Accrington) son of Mr. Wilfred Briggs, watchmaker, Blackburn-road, reported missing. Formerly employed at Howard and Bullough's.

PTE. R. W. JACKSON (Accrington) in a Liverpool hospital, suffering from shrapnel wounds in left arm and fingers, he was prior to the war employed at Messrs. Howard and Bullough's, and lived at 57, Richmond Hill-street.

LANCE-CORPL. E. SHARPLES (Accrington) a moulder at Howard and Bullough's, aged 27, in hospital abroad, wounded, expects to be in England shortly.

Local newspapers

Local newspapers can tell us a lot about local soldiers. Look at the picture on this page. The photographs are all of Accrington Pals. These men joined a Pals regiment so that they could fight next to their friends. The caption under each photograph tells us a lot about them.

Part of the Accrington Observer and Times. This newspaper was published on 22nd July, 1916.

We can find out what hospitals there were in the area, and where the men worked before they joined the Accrington Pals.

15

Children in the past

School photographs nowadays

Have you ever had your photograph taken at school? Perhaps the **photographer** took a picture of just you. Or perhaps the photographer took a picture of your whole class or even your whole school.

In years to come, other children will be able to look at these photographs. They will know what you looked like then, and what sorts of clothes children wore to school. If the photograph was taken in your classroom or in your playground, they will know what playgrounds and classrooms were like when you were at school.

Old school photographs

You may be able to find photographs of children who went to your school many years ago. If your family have lived in the same place for a long time, you may be able to spot your mother or father in an old school photograph. If your family have lived in the same place for a very long time, perhaps you can spot your grandparents. Whether you know the people in the photograph or not, you can still find out a lot about schools and children in those days.

Look at this old school photograph. What can you find out about girls' school clothes? Can you find out anything about what lessons were like?

This photograph of a lesson was taken sometime between 1898 and 1900.

School log books

Since about the 1840s, all schools have kept a school log-book. A log-book is a sort of **diary**. These school log-books tell us a lot about what happened in schools. On each day, the head teacher wrote down what had happened that day. For example, the head teacher wrote down whether the school had any visitors and who they were; whether there was an **epidemic** of measles which kept a lot of children at home; or whether farmers' children were allowed time off to help with the harvest.

School admission registers

These registers tell us a lot about the children. They tell us their names and ages, and the date on which they started school. They tell us the name of each child's father, and sometimes the name of the child's mother, too. They tell us when the child left school, and what each child went on to do – they may have taken a job or moved on to another school.

Kelly and Mark are looking at a log-book from their own school. This one was written in the 1920s.

LOOK OUT

Does your own school have log-books and admission registers from the past?

Hilda and the birthday book

Talking to Mum

Janet wanted to find out about the older people in her family and the places where they lived. Janet's own memories about her family began when she was a small child in the 1940s. Her mother was born in 1901, in the year Queen Victoria died. Janet went to talk to her Mum.

This photograph shows Elizabeth Walton's birthday book. It was given to her as a birthday present in 1884, when she was 23 years old.

THE ILLUSTRATED BIRTHDAY TEXT BOOK LONGFELLOW

Hilda's memories

Hilda, Janet's Mum, was nearly 90 years old. She told Janet about being a child in the 1900s. Hilda grew up in Whickham, a village in County Durham. She talked about the first time she saw a car, and how everyone in the village came out to look at this strange new way of travelling.

What did they leave behind?

Hilda and Janet found old photographs and special certificates, and then they discovered a small, black book. Inside the cover was written: 'E Walton, 13th April, 1884'. That was the name of Hilda's mother when she was young. This book was her **birthday book**.

LOOK OUT

Everyone has memories. You do not have to be 90 years old to have memories.

You could talk to people in your family and find out about their memories.

Sorting out old photographs

Some of the photographs Hilda and Janet found were over a hundred years old, but Hilda knew the names of all the people in the pictures. She put the photographs in time-order to help Janet understand the family's history. She started with pictures of herself and worked backwards to the pictures of her grandparents.

Investigating the birthday book

They discovered that Elizabeth's birthday book was a record of the whole family. She started writing in it on her 23rd birthday in 1884. For the rest of her life she wrote down the birthday of everyone in the family. Janet asked questions about all the people in the birthday book, and Hilda remembered many family stories from long ago. All this information helped Janet to make a **family tree**.

This shows Hilda in her pushchair in 1902. You can also see where Elizabeth recorded in her birthday book the day Hilda was born.

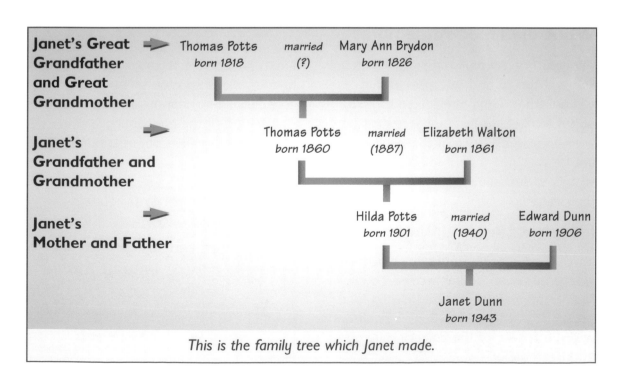

Janet's Great Grandfather and Great Grandmother → Thomas Potts born 1818 *married* (?) Mary Ann Brydon born 1826

Janet's Grandfather and Grandmother → Thomas Potts born 1860 *married* (1887) Elizabeth Walton born 1861

Janet's Mother and Father → Hilda Potts born 1901 *married* (1940) Edward Dunn born 1906

Janet Dunn born 1943

This is the family tree which Janet made.

Discovering Grandfather Tom

This photograph of Axwell Park Colliery was taken when Grandfather Tom worked there. The boy in the photograph might be Hilda's brother.

What did Hilda remember?

Thomas Potts was Janet's grandfather. She wanted to find out more about Grandfather Tom. She talked to Hilda about him. Hilda remembered that he worked in a **colliery** in the village, but he was not a coal-miner. He paid wages to the miners for the coal they mined.

Investigating buildings

Janet went to investigate the place where her grandfather worked, but found that the colliery had closed long ago. The buildings had been demolished and the tracks of the colliery railway had been pulled up.

Next, Janet went to the library and the local museum to look through the collections of old photographs there. This is one of the photographs she found. It was taken about a hundred years ago.

LOOK OUT

Look out for places where people in your family used to work.
Ask questions about where they went to school.

This is Grandfather Tom's marriage certificate. The photograph of Grandfather Tom was taken in 1887. This was the year of Queen Victoria's Golden Jubilee.

Clues from written sources

On this page you can see a photograph of Grandfather Tom's marriage certificate. It told Janet when he was born and where he lived when he was a young man. He married Elizabeth in 1887.

It also told Janet about Grandfather Tom's father. He was called Thomas Potts, too. He lived with his family at Delaval Farm House in the village of Benwell in Northumberland. But he was not a farmer. He was the manager in charge of Delaval Colliery.

Asking for help at the library

Your local history library probably has a good collection of sources to help you find out about your own family histories. Janet went to the library to look at the **census** returns for the village of Benwell in 1871. She looked through the list of houses in the village until she found Delaval Farm House.

There she found more evidence about Grandfather Tom. He was ten years old in 1871, but he was not a school boy. He was a **pupil teacher** at Benwell School. Janet made a time-line of his life story.

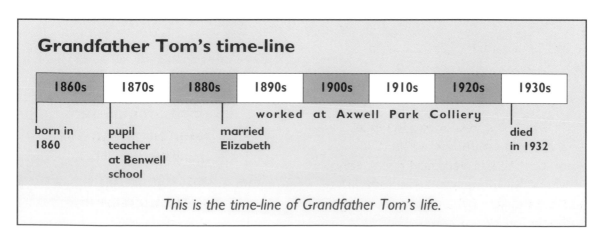

Grandfather Tom's time-line

1860s	1870s	1880s	1890s	1900s	1910s	1920s	1930s

worked at Axwell Park Colliery

born in 1860

pupil teacher at Benwell school

married Elizabeth

died in 1932

This is the time-line of Grandfather Tom's life.

Families on the move

Do all families move?

Some families stay in the same town or village for a very long time. Other families have moved from one place to another. Some people have lived in several different places. Have you lived in more than one place?

Adults often move to a place where there is a job for them, so that they can earn money and look after their families. People in the past did this, too.

Clues from the census

Janet read the **census** returns in the library. She noticed that every member of Grandfather Tom's family was born in a different village. The Potts family had certainly not stayed in the same community.

This gravestone records the year Thomas Potts died. The **birthday book** records the year he was born.

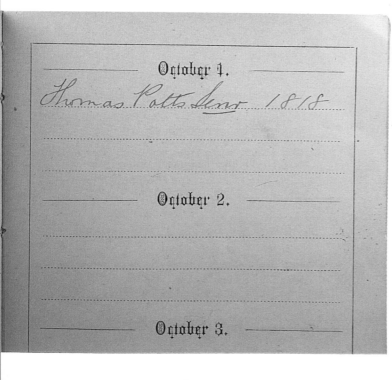

LOOK OUT

There might be a story of a family journey in your family. If there is, you could follow your family journey on a map. It might be a map of Britain or a map of the world.

This drawing was made before cameras were invented. It shows the place where wagons from Thomas Potts' coal-mines brought coal to the ships. The coal was on its way to London.

The beginning of the story

Grandfather Tom's father was also called Thomas Potts. Janet wanted to find out about Thomas's life story.

The census showed that he was born in the tiny village of Chollerton in the hills of Northumberland. The birthday book told Janet that his date of birth was 1818. Then she searched an old church register to find the day Thomas was taken to church to be **baptized**. She found Thomas's name and the name of his father, Joseph, who worked on a farm in Chollerton.

When Thomas was a man

Janet also found out from the census that by the 1840s, Thomas, his wife Mary Ann and their children lived in another part of Northumberland, far from the hills. They moved from village to village. Each village was crowded with houses and coal-mines.

Why did Thomas leave the hills to work in the mines? Janet read a book about the history of this area. She discovered that people left these hills because there were not enough jobs for them. When the railways came, new coal-mines opened in places where there was coal underground. People moved to these places to find work.

The end of the journey

Thomas kept moving to find better jobs. That is why his children were born in different villages. Eventually, he moved to Benwell, near the River Tyne, to be in charge of coal-mines there.

Finding the Dawson family

Who was Ellis Dawson?

Ellis Dawson was Rosemary's Dad. She wanted to find out where he was born and everything she could about his family. But Ellis had died in 1958, so Rosemary could not ask him anything.

Family memories

Rosemary asked her Mum what she remembered. Rosemary's Mum, Con, told her that Ellis had come from Manchester. His parents (Rosemary's grandparents), were both dead.

Rosemary's Grandma had died in about 1945, and her Grandad in about 1948. Con said that Rosemary's Dad had had two brothers, called Harry and Charlie. But both the brothers had died, too. There was no one left to ask. Con gave Rosemary a photograph of her Dad which was taken when he was about six months old.

*This is the photograph Con gave to Rosemary. Rosemary's Dad, Ellis, is about six months old. The picture was taken by the **photographer** F Danby, who worked in Radcliffe, in the city of Manchester.*

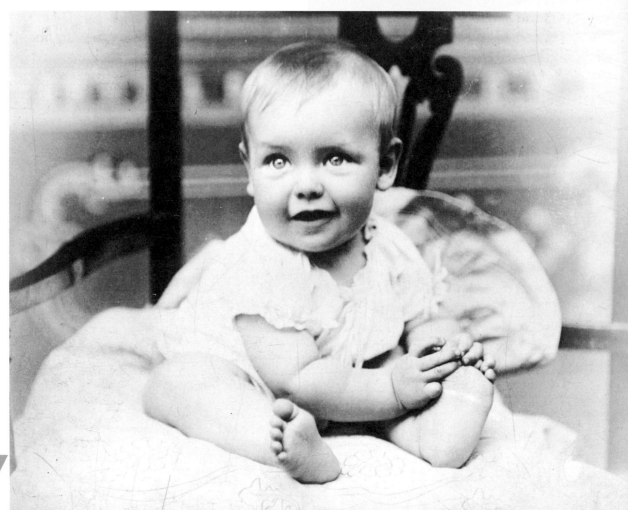

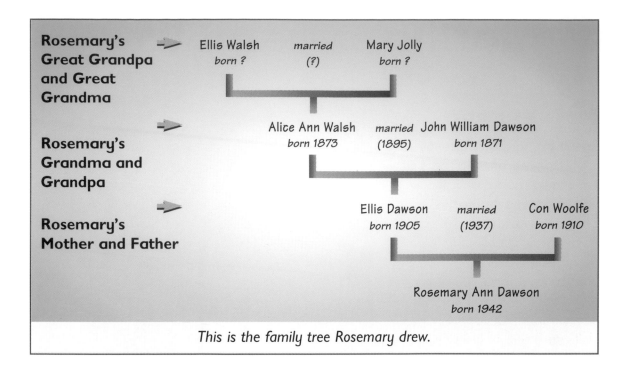

Rosemary's Great Grandpa and Great Grandma →
Ellis Walsh
born ?

married (?)

Mary Jolly
born ?

Rosemary's Grandma and Grandpa →
Alice Ann Walsh
born 1873

married (1895)

John William Dawson
born 1871

Rosemary's Mother and Father →
Ellis Dawson
born 1905

married (1937)

Con Woolfe
born 1910

Rosemary Ann Dawson
born 1942

This is the family tree Rosemary drew.

Birth certificate

Rosemary knew that her Dad was born on 5th December, 1905. She wrote to **St Katherine's House** in London, and got a copy of his birth certificate. From this she discovered that Ellis' mother was called Alice Ann and that his father was called John William. The birth certificate also said that when Ellis was born, the family were living at 28 Beech Street, Radcliffe, Manchester.

Marriage certificate

Rosemary worked out that her Grandma and Grandad Dawson must have been married at some time in the 1890s. She got a copy of their marriage certificate. From this she found out that they were married on 16th July, 1895. When they got married, John William was a grocer's assistant at the Co-op and Alice Ann worked in a cotton mill as a cotton warper.

Alice Ann's father, who was also culled Ellis, was dead when Alice Ann and John William married. He had been a journeyman cloth-finisher, and so had John William's father. Perhaps they had worked together in the same mill.

Family tree

Rosemary decided to draw a **family tree** to show how everybody she had discovered was related to each other.

LOOK OUT

What was the Co-op, a cotton warper and a journeyman cloth finisher?

Martha on the move

Family memories

Rosemary had a different problem with another part of her family. Too many people had too many memories! Everyone knew that Rosemary's great-grandmother, Martha, had lived to be nearly 100 years old. They knew that she and her husband, George Crane, had run a pub in London, and that she had worked as a **maid** before she got married.

But Rosemary's great-aunt Rose, who was one of Martha's daughters, told a different story. She said that Martha told her she had worked in fields when she was a little girl, and had eaten raw turnips when she was hungry. This did not seem to tie up with living in London!

Checking things out

Rosemary found out that Martha married George Crane in 1876. They married in Islington in London. Before that she lived at Denmark Grove, Islington. Martha had worked as a maid to Mr Steels, of Macclesfield Lodge, Hammersmith, London. But there did not seem to be a connection with the countryside at all.

Rosemary went to look for Denmark Grove. The address had stayed the same, but Martha never lived in this house. It is far too modern.

Parish registers

In 1837 Parliament passed a law that said all people's births, marriages and deaths had to be written down in official government registers. Before that, every parish church kept registers. The parish **priest** wrote down the names of everyone who had been **baptized**, married or buried in his church. But not all parish priests got things right. Another problem is that hundreds of parish registers have been lost over time.

Sometimes, when babies were baptized, the priest gave the baby's parents a special certificate. Rosemary found Martha's **baptismal certificate**. It said that Martha had been baptized in Datchworth, Hertfordshire. Perhaps this was the country connection!

Rosemary went to Datchworth Parish Church. There, she read the parish registers. She discovered that Martha had been born on 7 August, 1849. Martha was the youngest in her family. She had older brothers called George, Thomas and James, and a sister called Emma. Her parents were Eliza and Edmund Carpenter. Rosemary worked back through the parish registers, finding Martha's uncles, aunts and cousins. She got as far back as 1725. In that year Lydia and Benjamin Carpenter had arrived in Datchworth with four children and had settled down.

LOOK OUT

Where is your parish church? Where are the parish registers? Are they in the church, your local library or record office?

A photograph of Martha, taken when she was a ladies' maid before she married George.

A Jewish family

George Woolf's will

Rosemary's Mum gave her a copy of a **will** made by George Woolf in 1850. George Woolf was Rosemary's great-great grandfather who had died in 1852. The will left nearly everything George owned to his son, Joseph. Joseph, so the will said, was a little boy at the time. But George's wife, Joseph's mother, was not mentioned at all. What had happened?

A marriage certificate

Rosemary wrote to St Katherine's House in London. She asked for a copy of George Woolf's marriage certificate.

When the certificate arrived, it told Rosemary a lot about her family. George was married on 28th September, 1842, and his wife was called Maria Mordecai. They had been married at George's home, which was 106 Shoe Lane in the City of London. If you look carefully at the certificate, you will see that both George and Maria were Jews.

Ashkenazic Jews

The word *Ashkenazic* is a Hebrew word meaning 'German'. In the 18th and 19th centuries lots of Jews came to Britain from Germany, Poland and Russia. They settled mainly in the East End of London, in Leeds and in Manchester. They formed their own communities.

George and Maria's marriage certificate.

CERTIFIED COPY OF AN ENTRY OF MARRIAGE

The fee for this certificate is 40p. When application is made by post, d handling fee is payable in addition.

Given at the GENERAL REGISTER OFFICE, SOMERSET HOUSE, LONDON

Application Number PAS 43498/41

Registration District City of London

1842. Marriage solemnized at 106 Shoe Lane in the — of West London in the City of London

No.	When married	Name and surname	Age	Condition	Rank or profession	Residence at the time of marriage	Father's name and surname	Rank or profession of father
1	September 28th	George Woolf	full	Bachelor	Accountant	Shoe Lane	Joseph Woolf	—
		Maria Mordecai	—	Spinster	—	20 John Street Waterloo Road	Jonas Mordecai	—

Married in the Congregation of the New Synagogue according to the Rites & Ceremonies of the German & Polish Jews by me

This marriage was solemnized between us, George Woolf / Maria Woolf — in the presence of us, Phasius / Moses Levy — Abm Barrett Reader / J L Lindenthal Registrar

CERTIFIED to be a true copy of an entry in the certified copy of a Register of Marriages in the District above mentioned.

Given at the GENERAL REGISTER OFFICE, SOMERSET HOUSE, LONDON, under the Seal of the said Office, the 24th day of August 1941.

MA 945307

This certificate is issued in pursuance of section 65 of the Marriage Act 1949. Sub-section (3) of that section provides that any certified copy of an entry purporting to be sealed or stamped with the seal of the General Register Office shall be received as evidence of the marriage to which it relates without any further or other proof of the entry, and no certified copy purporting to have been given in the said Office shall be of any force or effect unless it is sealed or stamped as aforesaid.

CAUTION:—Any person who (1) falsifies any of the particulars on this certificate, or (2) uses a falsified certificate as true knowing it to be false, is liable to prosecution.

Given at the GENERAL REGISTER OFFICE,
SOMERSET HOUSE, LONDON.

Application Number....PAS 9254/2/71

REGISTRATION DISTRICT — West London

1849. DEATH in the Sub-district of West London in the City of London.

No.	When and where died	Name and surname	Sex	Age	Occupation	Cause of death	Signature, description, and residence of informant	When registered	Signature of registrar
Columns :— 1	2	3	4	5	6	7	8	9	
100	Eighteenth June 1849 106 Shoe Lane St. Brides	Maria Woolf	Female	32 years.	Wife of George Woolf Accountant.	Diarrhoea 8 days Cholera 4 days Premature Labour 32 hours Exaustion Certified.	G. Woolf Present at the Death 106 Shoe Lane London.	Nineteenth June 1849	William Nason Registrar

Maria's death certificate.

The 1851 census

When George made his will in 1850, his address was 106 Shoe Lane, London. Rosemary looked at the 1851 census for Shoe Lane. She discovered that George was living there with his son, Joseph, who was a child. A housekeeper, Elizabeth Bradley, was looking after them. But where was Joseph's mother?

Cholera

Rosemary guessed that Maria had died between her marriage in 1842 and the census in 1851. She got Maria's death certificate. This shows that she died on 18th June, 1849. She died because she caught the dreadful **disease**, **cholera**.

There were **epidemics** of cholera in Britain 1832–3, 1848–9, 1853–4, and again in 1866. Cholera could kill a healthy person in two days, and until the 1860s, no one knew how or why. In 1864 Louis Pasteur discovered that germs caused diseases like cholera.

LOOK OUT

Do people still catch cholera today? How is it cured?

Glossary

aisle a wide space between the shelves of goods for sale in a supermarket

architect a person who plans and designs buildings

baptismal certificate a certificate given to a child's parents when the child is baptized

baptize when a priest touches a person with holy water to show they belong to a church

birthday book a book in which a person writes down the dates of birthdays of friends and relations

census a count of all the people, made every ten years

cholera a disease

colliery a coal-mine

diary a book in which a person writes down what happens to them each day

disease an illness

enumerators men who, in the 19th century, were sent by the government to find out who lived in every house in the country

epidemic when a lot of people catch the same disease at the same time

family tree a diagram showing how people in a family are related to each other

famous well known

graveyard the ground around a church where people are buried

imaginary not real, but thought up by someone

maid a woman or girl who is a servant

mayor the person elected to lead a local council

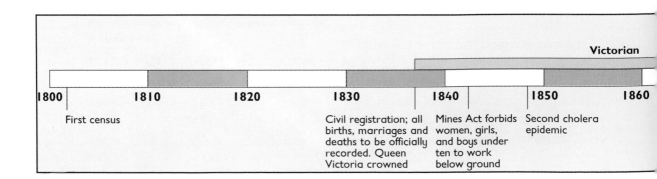

Victorian

| 1800 | 1810 | 1820 | 1830 | 1840 | 1850 | 1860 |

First census

Civil registration; all births, marriages and deaths to be officially recorded. Queen Victoria crowned

Mines Act forbids women, girls, and boys under ten to work below ground

Second cholera epidemic

memorial something which is put up in memory of a person or event

Parliament the House of Commons and House of Lords which, with the monarch, makes laws

Pals regiment special regiments, usually linked with a town, which were formed during the First World War (1914–18), and which the young men in that town joined

photographer a person who takes photographs

plaster a mixture of lime, sand and water, which is spread on walls to make a hard surface

priest a person who runs a church and teaches people about God

pupil teacher someone who is learning to be a teacher

regiment part of an army

statue a model of a person or animal, usually found outside and usually made of something hard, such as marble, stone or metal

St Katherine's House a place which holds copies of all the country's birth and death certificates

street directory a book listing all the jobs that were done in a town or a city, the names of the people who did the work, and the addresses where they worked

will a document saying what a person wants to happen to their belongings when they die

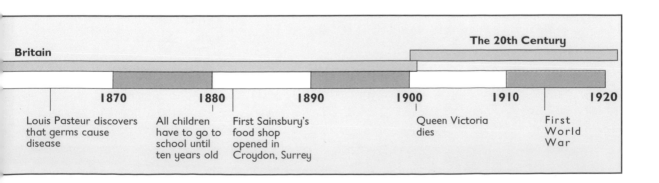

Britain

The 20th Century

1870   1880   1890   1900   1910   1920

Louis Pasteur discovers that germs cause disease

All children have to go to school until ten years old

First Sainsbury's food shop opened in Croydon, Surrey

Queen Victoria dies

First World War

Index

Numbers in plain type (27) refer to the text. Numbers in italic type *(27)* refer to a caption or a picture.

Accrington Pals   15, *15*
architect   6
army regiments   14, 15
Ashkenazic Jews   28
Axwell Park Colliery   *20*

baptismal certificates   27
Benwell   21, 23
birth certificates   25
birthday book   18, *18*, 19, *19, 22,* 23
Bradford   4
Brownies   *5*
buildings, important   6
Burnley   9

censuses   10, *10*, 11, *11*, 21, 22, 23
children   5, 12
   at school   16–17
   working in coal mines   13
   cholera   12, 29
Chollerton   23
city communities   4
coal-mining   13, 20, 23, *23*
coal-mining disaster   13
collieries   20, *20*, 21
Colyton   6, *6*
communities   4–5
   city communities   4
   things that happen   4, 5
   village communities   4
   what they are   4
Crane, George and Martha   26–7, *27*

Datchworth   27
Dawson, Ellis   24–5, *24*
death certificates   29, *29*
diseases   12, 29

enumerators   11
epidemics   12, 17, 29

families   10, 12
   family histories   18–29
   a Jewish family   28–9
   journeys   22–3
family shops   8, *8*
family trees   19, *19*, 25, *25*
famous and important people   6–7, *7*
festivals   4, *4*, 5
First World War   14
'flu   12
foundation stones   6

government   10, 11
gravestones   12, *12*, 13, 22

Habergham Eaves   *11*
Harrogate   7
houses   10, *10*

Jewish family   28–9

Kenton   *12*

local halls   5, *5*
local history library   21
London   *10,* 26, *26,* 28, 29

Malton   *8*
Manchester   24, *24,* 25
marriage certificates   21, *21*, 25, 28, *28*

memorials   13, *13,* 14, *14*

newspapers, local   15, *15*
Notting Hill carnival   4

Padiham   *14*
Pals regiments   14, 15, *15*
parish registers   27
Parliament   13, 27
Pasteur, Louis   29
Potts family   18–21, 22, 23

St Katherine's House   25, 28
school admission registers   17
school log-books   17, *17*
school photographs   16, *16*
Second World War   14
shops and supermarkets   8
Silkstone   13, *13*
soldiers   14, 15, *15*
statues   7, *7*
street directories   8, 9

Victoria, Queen   7, *7,* 18, 21
village communities   4

war memorials   14, *14*
Whickham   18
wills   28, 29
Woolf, George and Maria   28–9, *28, 29*
working people   8, 9, 12, 13, 20, 21, 22, 23, 25, 26

People and Communities

LOCAL STUDIES IN HISTORY AND GEOGRAPHY

Rosemary Rees

Janet Withersby

Heinemann

First published in Great Britain by Heinemann Library, Halley Court, Jordan Hill, Oxford OX2 8EJ
a division of Reed Educational and Professional Publishing Ltd

OXFORD FLORENCE PRAGUE MADRID ATHENS MELBOURNE AUCKLAND KUALA LUMPUR
SINGAPORE TOKYO IBADAN NAIROBI KAMPALA JOHANNESBURG GABORONE
PORTSMOUTH NH CHICAGO MEXICO CITY SAO PAULO

Designed by Aricot Vert Design

Illustrations by Judy Allen-Storey

Printed in the UK by Jarrold Book Printing Ltd, Thetford

00 99 98 97 96

10 9 8 7 6 5 4 3 2 1

ISBN 0 431 07895 5

This title is also available in a hardback library edition (ISBN 0 431 07892 0).

British Library Cataloguing in Publication Data

Rees, Rosemary, 1942 –

   People and communities – (Local studies in history and geography)

   1. Community – Juvenile literature

   2. Human settlements – Juvenile literature

   I. Title II. Withersby, Janet

   307

Acknowledgements

The Publishers would like to thank the following for permission to reproduce photographs:
ACE Photo Agency: p.10; Beamish Photographic Library: p.20;
Hatton Gallery, University of Newcastle upon Tyne: p.23; Katz Pictures, Stuart Nicol: p.4;
Mansell Collection: p.16; Mrs Norah Mash: p.27; Rosemary Rees: pp.24, 26;
Roger Scruton: pp.5-8, 12-14, 17; Phil Withersby: pp.18, 19, 21, 22

"The Wounded Pals" reproduced with kind permission of The Accrington Observer and Times.

The Lancashire Street Directory reproduced with kind permission of Burnley Reference Library,
Lancashire County Library.

1851 Census reproduced from The Public Record Office with the permission of The Controller of Her Majesty's
Stationery Office, © Crown Copyright, ref. no: HO 107/2252.

Cover photograph reproduced with permission of J. Woodcock, Reflections Photo Library.

Our thanks to Jane Shuter for her comments in the preparation of this book.

Every effort has been made to contact copyright holders of any material reproduced in this book.
Any omissions will be rectified in subsequent printings if notice is given to the Publisher.